GROW A GARDEN!

MAKER COMICS

GROW A GARDEN!

Alexis Frederick-Frost

:01
First Second
New York

Gardening isn't without some risks.
Don't let sunburn, bugbites, or other
injuries spoil your fun.

You can get sunburned even if it's overcast, so apply sunscreen
with SPF 15 or higher before going outside. A hat with a wide
brim can help keep the sun off your face and neck.

Protect yourself from bugbites by using bug repellent.

Invest in a good pair of gardening gloves to help avoid skin
irritation, cuts, and blisters! Wash your hands after gardening
whether you wear gloves or not. Dirt can be pretty dirty!

When using garden tools, make sure to point them away from
other people and keep the digging ends close to the ground.

Always be cautious when using power tools! Ask for help
from an adult when using a hand drill or other devices.
Wear safety goggles and sturdy closed-toe shoes
when operating power tools.

Lift heavy objects (like bags of soil)
with a two-stage lift:

1) Bend your knees and grab the heavy
   object, holding it close to your body.

2) Keep your back straight and push up
   with your legs.

If the object is too heavy, see if someone
else can help you carry it. Use a wheelbarrow to
move heavy loads from place to place.

If you plan on spending most of the day outside
in hot weather, make sure you stay hydrated.
Drink plenty of water and avoid
sugary beverages.

Geez, Will is in a bad mood today.

I think he's nervous about being in a new school.

Hurry!

This place *is* much nicer than middle school. Look, there's a picture painted on the ceiling!

It's like we're inside a comic!

Sorry we're late...

The bus was a tortoise.

You just made it. Class is about to start.

HUF HUF HUF HUF HUF

NEW STUDEN CHECK-IN

NEW STUDENT

WELCOME TO GARDEN GNOME

Student orientation is in the next room.

I believe Mr. Butternut is the only teacher still accepting new students.

Thanks!

CHECK-

NEW STUDENT

Why get your hands dirty when you can take my class and learn about exotic orchids in the greenhouse?

I hope our teacher is cool.

DIRT

NEW STUDENT

Uhh... Excuse me, are you Mr. Butternut?

How insulting! I'm Mr. Thorn. I have nothing in common with that dirt brain.

He wastes his time digging in the garden like a lowly earthworm.

I research rare, exotic, and dangerous flora. He can't even begin to appreciate my botanical genius.

Gnomes must look beyond the garden to find true greatness. I teach about plants worthy of study.

7

Look around. Among this trash is *treasure*!

Oooh... I love treasure hunts.

You must learn what is rubbish and what is useful.

Bones, greasy pizza boxes, cheese, and stuff that can't be recycled does belong in the trash...

...but stuff like vegetable peels, old salad greens, shredded paper, coffee grounds, and tea bags can be used...

TEA

...to make valuable *compost*. Mixing compost into garden soil helps plants grow.

How?

It improves soil by adding *organic* material to it.

*Organic can also mean that a plant was grown without pesticides or synthetic fertilizers.

Wow!!! That was *awesome!*

Mr. B has some superhero-level moves.

That was a really fun treasure hunt.

I can't believe I'm stuck taking out the trash.

Hello there, young gnome.

Mr. Toad, can you teach me how to turn this stuff into compost?

Of course. I'm toad-ally happy to teach you!

Are you joking?

Let's *jump* right in!

SLAP

First, we need to find a *compost bin* to hold the organic material you've collected.

It can be simple, like this one made from chicken wire held together with cable ties.

However, a bin with a lid will help keep pests away.

This smells like dinner to me!

Luckily, you can make a plastic trash can into a pest-resistant compost bin.

12

MAKE YOUR OWN COMPOST BIN

With a few modifications, this thirty-two-gallon plastic trash can will become a compost bin.

A latching top and wheels are nice features, but any large plastic can with a lid will work. Dark-colored containers will absorb heat from the sun and speed up the composting process.

latches

wheels

You will need a drill, a one-inch drill bit, a ruler...

a few bricks to raise the bin off the ground...

and bungee cords to keep the lid secure.

Remember:
SAFETY FIRST!

Power drills can be dangerous.

Never use one without adult supervision.

Always wear eye and ear protection when using power tools.

Start with a three-inch base layer of carbon-rich material like dry leaves, shredded newspaper, or straw. Then add a three-inch layer of nitrogen-rich stuff.

Alternate adding thin layers of carbon and of nitrogen material. When you're out of stuff to add, cover the last layer with soil or dry leaves.

soil
nitrogen
carbon
nitrogen
carbon
nitrogen

Spray the pile with a little water. It should be slightly damp, not soaked.

Not too wet!

Aaaaahh...

I'm decomposing!

It takes many months for things to decompose. But still, gnomes are not on the list of things to put in a compost bin!

I'd like to get out of here sooner rather than later.

Climb on. We'll pull you up!

Thanks.

Bacteria, fungi, and other microorganisms will break down the organic material in the compost bin.

The holes let in oxygen, which aerobic bacteria need to live. The bin might get warm to the touch as they make compost.

Feel the burn.

As the organic material decomposes, it compresses. Oxygen levels in the compost will drop and anaerobic bacteria that don't need oxygen to thrive will take over, producing stinky waste.

STINK

To avoid a smelly situation, mix the bin's contents every month with a shovel. This aerates the compost and adds oxygen for aerobic bacteria.

Remember, to keep your compost from getting stinky:

1. Mix it every month.
2. Add equal amounts of green and brown stuff.
3. Avoid adding meat and other animal products.
4. Keep the lid closed.

Compost is ready when it looks brown and crumbly, and no large pieces of food are visible.

So basically it looks like dirt?

Yes. I started this bin last year. It should be filled with finished compost by now.

This bin is from a store. The door at the bottom makes it easy to remove finished compost.

Cool.

This does look like dirt. I can't tell that it was food.

Uh... What's that?

Something is moving in here!

SHAKE

ARRGGHH!!!

A worm!

Awesome!

18

I think something is caught in its throat. What did you eat, you silly worm?

Whoa, it's really stuck in there.

BURP

Oh, gross.

What is it?

Buried treasure?

I can't tell. There's too much drool.

I know worms have big appetites, but this is really strange.

It looks like a weird thing to eat.

You're right, Basil. Some earthworms can eat their weight in food each day.

They are one type of macroorganism that you might find in your compost pile.

Certain macroorganisms, like sow bugs, millipedes, and worms, eat organic materials. Their excrement is digested by bacteria and turned into nutrients for plants.

Nasty! Can we go get clean now?

Okay! See you later when you're ready to fertilize the garden!

Bye!

Hey, Violet. Can I look at that thing you found?

Sure.

It's some sort of weird metallic medallion.

Which is strange because metal is recyclable and doesn't belong in compost.

Sorry!!!
I didn't see
you there.

Pay
attention to
where you're
going!!

Ugh... You're filthy!
What have you been doing?
Rolling around in mud like a
little piglet?

Actually, I
learned how to
make compost.

Whoa...
I am sooo
glad I'm not in
your class.

Mr. Thorn took
my class to the
greenhouse to see
an orchid with a
special flower that
attracts bees.

Bees visit the
orchid because
the flower kinda
looks like
another bee.

They end up
pollinating
the plant by
mistake!

Eucera
bee

flower
disguised as a
bee

Ophrys apifera
"bee orchid"

This distraction is keeping me from important work.

I don't have time to deal with delinquent students and their dirty pets.

Your behavior is unacceptable but hardly surprising considering your teacher.

If I was in charge, all of you, *including* that soil skull Butternut, would be expelled immediately!

But the worm is so cute. Can we keep him?

No way! I can't get expelled... I just got here!

Aww... Come on, Will, he's nice. It'll be our secret. Mr. Thorn will never know.

Let's check to see if the library has any books about caring for pet worms.

Wahoo! Another treasure hunt!

I don't think the medallion is a movie prop!

Whoa! We're somewhere beneath the school.

Students aren't supposed to be in the library access tunnel.

Please don't expel us. We don't know what happened.

Don't worry, little buddy. I'm here to help! As they say: Together we...

Oh, beans. I always forget the next part...

Go?

Glow?

Row?

Together we *grow*? The Green Hat Gnomes' catch-phrase?

That's right.

I *never* remember the whole thing.

I guess that's why I'm stuck down here while those gnomes are planting gardens and saving the world.

Wait, wait, wait. Hold on just one second. The Green Hat Gnomes are real?

Of course they are. I work for them.

A bit of advice: Not everything is what it seems. Come on, I'll show you what I mean.

You may think I'm just a small naked mole rat, **but** my family has been working with Team Green for generations.

We stay out of the limelight, so you'll never see us in a comic or a movie.

Although I think *The Adventures of Marvelous Marvin* would be a pretty good film.

The Green Hat Gnomes get all their seeds from us.

The time Super Sprout needed seeds for an octopus garden under the sea—she got them from us.

We also provide seeds to other garden gnomes, including students.

You know, without seeds, garden gnomes wouldn't exist. Because a garden gnome with no garden is *gnome*body!

Can we have some of your seeds?

35

*Tomato plants can either be **determinate** or **indeterminate**. **Determinate** plants stop growing when they reach a certain height while **indeterminate** varieties will grow until they are killed by frost.

Slow-growing crops need a long growing season to produce a harvest.

Gardeners raising these crops in regions with a short growing season have to start their seeds indoors and transplant seedlings into the garden after the last spring frost.

As you become a more experienced gardener, you'll get familiar with your local growing season. Keep a gardening journal to record which seeds grew well and when you planted them.

Fortunately, the first-time gardener can look online for information about the growing season in their region.

Search for websites that list first and last frost dates by zip code.

GNOMEgle
SEARCH

But the internet connection is pretty bad down here in the tunnels. So sometimes I have to use a map.

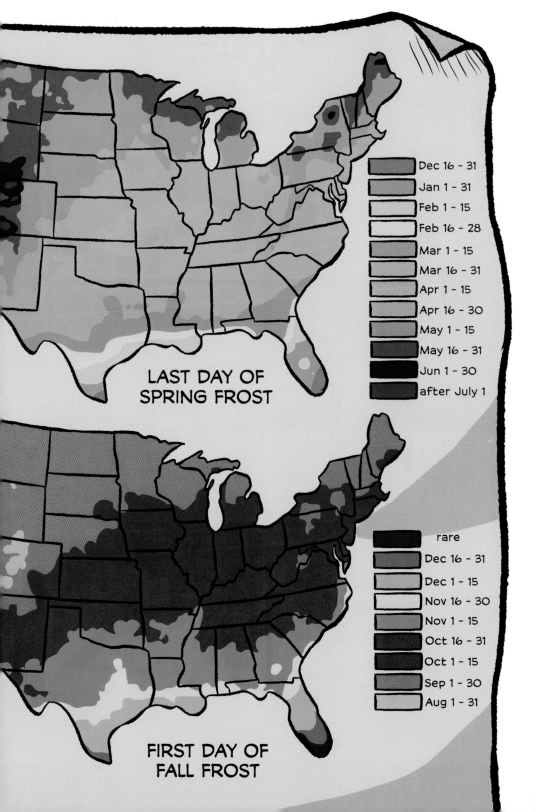

LAST DAY OF
SPRING FROST

Dec 16 – 31
Jan 1 – 31
Feb 1 – 15
Feb 16 – 28
Mar 1 – 15
Mar 16 – 31
Apr 1 – 15
Apr 16 – 30
May 1 – 15
May 16 – 31
Jun 1 – 30
after July 1

rare
Dec 16 – 31
Dec 1 – 15
Nov 16 – 30
Nov 1 – 15
Oct 16 – 31
Oct 1 – 15
Sep 1 – 30
Aug 1 – 31

FIRST DAY OF
FALL FROST

I hope this works in reverse.

We're going up!

We made it!

That was close. I hope Marvin is okay.

He seemed able to take care of himself.

!

BUMP

Wrigley! You waited for us. I'm so glad to see you.

Who is making all that noise?

What is going on in here?

Uh, we're... just...ah... researching?

Seeds and stuff.

Wait a second. Is that a worm?

Yeah...

Ah, but not a bookworm, I see.

You are good, yes?

No eating my books. Or else...

I'll eat you!

Ha, ha, ha... I'm joking. He's a cutie.

So tell me about these seeds you have.

45

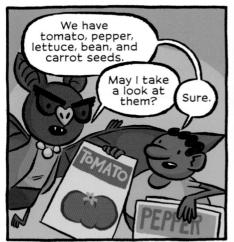

We have tomato, pepper, lettuce, bean, and carrot seeds.

May I take a look at them?

Sure.

Hmm... You should plant the pepper and tomato seeds soon.

But it's still cold outside.

And Marvin said seeds won't grow in the cold.

I don't suggest putting them outside yet.

You should start them inside.

Most tomatoes and peppers are native to the southern part of America...

where the growing season is longer and warmer than it is here.

But we can extend the growing season by starting seeds inside weeks before the weather warms up here in Gnomeville.

sweet peppers

tomatoes

Some seeds, like lettuce seeds, can be started indoors or planted outside in the spring.

Lettuce

Sowing Instructions: Direct sow or transplant in early spring as soon as the soil is workable. Direct Seeding: Plant seeds 1/8 inch deep, in rows 10 to 12 inches apart. When plants develop true leaves, thin to 6 to 10 inches between sprouts. Transplants: Sow inside 3 to 4 weeks...

Root vegetables, like carrots, don't like being moved and should be sown directly in the garden.

CARROTS

But both pepper and tomato seeds need to be planted indoors three to eight weeks before the last spring frost.

According to Marvin's map, that's this week.

But how can you plant seeds indoors?

You plant them in pots. Garden supply stores sell peat pots or plastic trays for starting seeds indoors.

But you can also plant seeds in recycled containers.

RECYCLE

I'm sure you can find something in the recycling bins outside.

Could you take these newspapers with you?

RECYCLE

I can't believe I'm doing this again.

Hey, Will! Whatcha doing?

I'm looking for the recycling.

We need some containers to start seeds in.

You've come to the right place.

That bin is full of plastic containers.

PAPER

PLASTIC

Another treasure hunt!

Uh-oh...

Aaahh!!!

Oooh... Here's a good one.

Don't worry about me. I'm okay!

Choose containers that are three to four inches deep and hold at least a half cup (about four ounces) of potting soil.

This yogurt container is the perfect size!

Plastic containers must have a top opening larger than its bottom. Otherwise, you won't be able to remove the seedling later. It will get stuck.

Just like my head...

Soak the recycled containers for fifteen minutes in distilled white vinegar with five percent acidity. Then give them a good scrub. This treatment won't sterilize the pots.

But it will kill some bacteria that can harm delicate seedlings.

Remember: **Safety first!**

Vinegar is a safe and natural cleaner. However, it can cause skin and eye irritation.

Provide ventilation (or go outside) if the smell bothers you.

Wash hands thoroughly with soap and water when finished.

After the containers are clean...

rinse them thoroughly with water.

Carefully poke holes in the bottom with a pencil or nail.

Drainage is very important!

Hey, Violet, do we have enough containers for all our seeds?

I don't think so.

No worries!

We can make more out of newspaper!

MAKE YOUR OWN SEED POT

from newspaper!

The materials you need are:

sheets of newspaper.

Don't use glossy magazine paper.

A small can to shape the newspaper pots. Be careful to avoid cutting yourself on any sharp edges left by the can opener.

And masking tape.

Step 1

Tear a sheet of newspaper in half along the fold.

Step 2

Fold the torn sheet in half lengthwise to make a long, narrow rectangle.

53

54

Wrigley! I didn't know you could speak.

I'm just getting my voice back after having that thing stuck in my throat.

My name is Sir Wigglesworth Slimyington the Third...

but you can still call me Wrigley.

I am somewhat of a soil connoisseur.

Is a connoisseur like a dinosaur?!

No, it means he knows a lot about soil.

As I was saying, garden soil is too heavy to be used in a container. It's full of rocks, clay, and other dense material that becomes compressed in a pot.

A pot filled with dirt does not drain well and often will become waterlogged.

Saturated soil can kill seeds and the roots of plants.

dense dirt

waterlogged

Even worse, soil from outside might contain mold spores, fungus, or bugs that could harm tender seedlings.

Errk!

55

Wise worms sow seeds in special growing medium specifically made for growing potted plants. It's often sold in bags labeled seedling mix or seed-starting potting mix.

This is nice!

SEEDLING START MIX

These mixtures have a fine texture, which is easier for new roots to grow through.

They also have been sterilized to destroy harmful bacteria and fungi.

That's good.

Dry seedling mix absorbs water slowly. Hydrate it by putting some in a separate container. Then add water to it. Wait a few minutes for the liquid to be absorbed before filling the pots with the moist mixture.

Add enough water for the potting mix to hold its shape when squeezed.

Too much water will make it muddy and too runny to use.

YES

NO

Step 1

To make potting mix, simply measure out an equal amount of each ingredient.

Don't worry about being too exact.

Use compost that has been screened to remove large pieces of organic material. Young roots will grow through the fine texture of screened compost more easily.

1 bucket of peat moss or coconut coir fiber

1 bucket of perlite

1 bucket of screened compost

It's best to use compost from a pile that got warm enough during decomposition to kill harmful fungi or wild seeds.

If your compost pile never got warm, or you don't have a compost bin, then buy organic compost to use instead.

I'm feeling hot, hot, *hot!*

Step 2

Mix the ingredients together in a large container.

Step 3

Add water and stir the ingredients to break up any dry clumps. Moist potting mix can get moldy when stored, so use it up!

You can customize this recipe to suit your needs. Experiment until you find the mix you like best.

Now we're ready to plant our seeds!

Fill the pots completely with potting mix. Then press the mix down about a half inch. The mix should be firm enough to support a plant...

...but loose enough for roots to grow through easily.

Make two shallow holes a quarter inch deep and a quarter inch apart near the center of the pot.

1/4 inch

Place a seed in each hole and cover with soil. Label each pot before you forget which type of seeds you sowed.

PEPPER

Two seeds will double the chance that a plant will grow.

If both seeds sprout, then we'll only keep one.

Pluck and discard the weakest sprout.

Seeds are *geotropic*, which means they use gravity to orient themselves. It doesn't matter how they're planted;

roots will grow down and the stem will grow upward.

I made it!

epicotyl
(stem above
cotyledon)

plumule
(plant shoot)

hypocotyl
(stem below
cotyledon)

radicle
(root)

cotyledon
(first leaves)

seed
coat

Each seed contains a dormant baby plant.

What makes it start to grow?

The two W's! Water and warmth.

In nature, a seed remains dormant during the cold winter.

Spring rain moistens the seed and softens its protective coat.

The sun warms the soil and the seed germinates.

Brrrr...

What does *germinate* mean?

I think it's an illness.

Ha ha! Germination is when a dormant seed begins growing.

Since we are planting seeds indoors, we are responsible for providing the water and warmth the seeds will need to germinate.

60

In general, seeds need temperatures above seventy-five degrees Fahrenheit during the day and sixty-five degrees at night to germinate.

← 75 degrees

← 65 degrees

That's warm, which is why the perfect place to start seeds is in a greenhouse!

Luckily, the school has one!

Let's take the tray of paper pots first. We will come back for the others.

The four of you can carry it together.

Greenhouses are made of glass or clear plastic.

The sun heats the air inside, warming it even in the winter.

sun rays

heat

heat

Hmm... For some reason, the door is locked.

Let's go to the cafeteria.

Wrigley, are you hungry again?

That's a great idea. The kitchen can be a good place to start seeds.

In fact, one of the best places is on top of the refrigerator.

But the fridge keeps stuff cold.

Yes...

...it *is* cold on the inside.

However, coils on the back or bottom of the refrigerator get warm during the cooling process.

The heat rises to the top of the refrigerator, creating slightly warmer air temperatures that help seeds germinate.

Weeks later

I can't believe how many comic books there are in the library.

Hey, is that Kara?

Thanks, kitty.

?

What?! She helped get that bottle off my head.

She's actually pretty nice.

Hey, everyone, look! The bagged seeds have sprouted!

I can see tiny roots.

It's time to move them into pots.

It's okay if some paper sticks to the sprout.

Some roots have grown into the paper towel.

So how are your seeds? Have they sprouted?

Yes, but we're running out of space for them.

Hmmm... I see.

This *is* a problem.

Seedlings need eight hours of direct sunlight or more a day.

Less than that and they'll grow thin and weak, stretching to find more light.

Light... I need more light...

A south-facing window will provide enough light for a few seedlings.

But you have too many sprouts. They need more space and light.

A grow shelf could provide the additional light they crave.

Does the school have one?

No, but we can make one ourselves!

Naked mole rats, assemble!

MAKE YOUR OWN Grow light SHELF

You called, boss?

You can make a great grow light setup from utility shelving and some fluorescent shop lights.

48-inch-wide shelves

You need one thirty-six- or forty-eight-inch-wide shelving unit.

And two shop lights with fluorescent bulbs.

Wire utility shelves are easy to hang shop lights from.

Plastic shelves are more affordable and work well, too.

A plug-in timer is useful. It will turn the lights on and off automatically.

T5-type fluorescent bulbs are the most efficient, but other types (T8 or T12), will work, too.

You also need a power strip to plug the lights into.

Step 1

Assemble the shelving unit following the manufacturer's instructions.

You can save money by reusing old shelving units that are past their prime.

Step 2

Install the fluorescent bulbs in the shop light fixtures. Get help if you don't feel comfortable doing it yourself.

Step 3

Hang the lights from the top shelf using their hangers and hooks.

We will adjust the chain length so the lights are four inches above the seedlings' top leaves.

Step 4

It's dangerous for water to come in contact with electricity. Place the power strip somewhere between twelve inches and three feet from the shelf, where it won't get wet.

power strip

timer

Keep away from water!

Step 5

Plug the lights into the power strip. Then plug the strip into the timer. Finally, plug the timer into an outlet. Set it to leave the lights on from 7 a.m. to 9 p.m.

There are many more boxes full of comics just like this one!

It will take us weeks to read them all!

Week 1

These old comics are pretty entertaining.

I told you Captain Compost was cool.

Week 2

Have you read the issue where he makes a super shovel out of a meteorite?

Wait till you see what it does.

Week 3

Whoa... He planted a garden on Mars!

The shovel gives him super gardening powers.

And he can use its otherworldly superpowers to control soil.

He's able to grow vegetables anywhere—even in the middle of a city.

I wish we had super gardening powers like that.

All you do is talk about comics. I can't handle it anymore.

Let's take a break and get some food.

You're always hungry, Wrigley.

I'm not hungry but the seedlings probably are. They've been growing for a while and need more food to continue.

During the first few weeks of their lives, seedlings use food stored in the seed to grow.

Those nutrients are gone by the time a seedling develops a second set of leaves, which are called "true leaves."

In order for seedlings to grow strong and healthy, they need to get more nutrients from the soil.

cotyledon
(First leaves to appear. Also called seed leaves.)

root

true leaves

seed leaves

I'm hungry.

Some seed mixes contain fertilizer, but many don't. You have to provide additional nutrients by using liquid fertilizer.

SEEDLING STARTING MIX

Fertilizers can either be synthetic, which have been manufactured from minerals and inorganic material, or organic, which come from plant or animal sources.

TOMATO GROW

I guess I'm just bad at growing stuff.

Gardening can be difficult.

What kind of garden gnome am I if I can't grow a garden?

We might be able to help.

Really? You'd do that for me?

Yeah, we're all garden gnomes, right?

And good gnomes should help each other out.

Like the Green Hat Gnomes say, "Together we *grow!*"

Let's look at these seedlings of yours.

Okay!

I put them by my bedroom window.

I water them every day before bed.

And I always have the radio on so they have something groovy to listen to.

This time use sterilized seedling potting soil...

...water less, and provide more light.

But I can't start over.

I've used up all my seeds.

I can't get more. There's a seed shortage for some reason.

That monster must have destroyed Marvin's supply.

Ssshhh...

We have extra seeds we could share.

That's true!

We haven't planted any of the lettuce seeds yet.

Yeah, we still have a few packages.

Good idea! Lettuce likes cool weather and can even survive a light frost. Its seeds can be sown outside three or four weeks before the last frost. Even earlier with a cold frame!

Cool weather is lovely.

Cold frames are like mini-greenhouses for a few plants.

They extend the growing season by capturing warmth from the sun and protecting plants from cold winds and weather.

They are small and relatively inexpensive and easy to build.

A simple one can be made from a window or storm door and some straw bales.

1. Gather together some straw bales and an unbroken storm door or window.

2. Arrange the straw bales around seedlings.

3. Prop the storm door or window against the straw bales.

enclosure created from straw bales

Don't use old windows or doors that might be covered with lead paint, which is very toxic and dangerous to handle, and can contaminate the soil.

I don't think we have enough room for a bunch of straw bales.

If space is limited, you can make a nifty cold frame from two plastic window well covers.

MAKE YOUR OWN

CoLD Frame

USING WINDOW WELL COVERS

Window well covers are used to prevent rain and snow from getting into basement window wells.

They come in a variety of sizes and are available at most home improvement stores.

For this project, you need two matching plastic bubble-type covers.

Use large ones with a width and height of at least fifteen inches.

15 inches high

48 inches long

17 inches wide

window well (with a cover)

You will also need five small spring clamps...

tent stakes or heavy bricks...

self-sticking 7/16-inch-thick, 3/4-inch-wide, 10-foot-long foam weather stripping...

...a hammer or rubber mallet...

...and a min-max thermometer, which is a special thermometer that records high and low temperatures.

Anyway, I'm going to take a picture every few hours.

At the end of the day, we can compare them to determine which area is the sunniest.

So we're going to be up here for six to eight hours.

Some areas only get sun in the morning or afternoon. This will help us find one that is sunny all day long.

It's a good thing I brought comics!

Nice!

I'd rather spend time with the beekeeper.

KNOCK KNOCK

BEEKEEPER

Whoa!

Hi there.

8:00 A.M.

11:00 A.M.

3:00 P.M.

6:00 P.M.

Hello there. How's it going?

I see you activated the sprinkler system.

FWOOSHHH

I'll turn it off for the moment, since there's not a garden here yet.

But how can we plant a garden here? There's enough sun but no soil.

How can I help?

Dug!

This stone courtyard is the only place that gets enough sun for a vegetable garden.

The rest of the area is too shady.

Hmmm, I see. Well, we can't dig up the courtyard.

But we could plant a container garden.

What's a container garden?

It's a garden where plants are grown in containers filled with potting mix instead of being planted in the ground. It's a great way to grow veggies if you have limited space.

What vegetables are you growing?

Lettuce to start.

Lettuce is a great container plant because it has shallow roots.

Leafy greens, radishes, and many herbs grow well in shallow containers like window boxes. Look for something six to seven inches deep.

7-inch-deep box

Other vegetables need more space to grow. Beans, peppers, rosemary, and squash can grow in five-gallon buckets or other containers that are at least fifteen inches deep.

Tomato plants have an extensive root system. A large storage bin or trash can that is at least sixteen inches deep will give the roots room to grow.

So we need to use different containers for different plants?

Yep! Luckily, you can grow a garden in all kinds of things.

Like an old tire or a barrel...

But certain things work better than others.

Larger containers are best.

They hold more soil, which can support large plants that grow more vegetables.

Plants in big containers don't need to be watered as often as plants in small ones.

And they are less likely to fall over in the wind.

But there's a downside: they're very heavy!

Pay attention to the materials the container is made of.

Wooden boxes or barrels look nice, but when they're filled with soil they will be too heavy to move.

Unglazed clay pots are pretty, but they are heavy and can break or dry out the soil.

Fabric grow bags are inexpensive and portable but may not appeal to everyone's sense of style.

100

A small plastic window box is a good choice for growing lettuce.

Make sure it fits underneath the cold frame.

We need more potting soil to fill it.

Make the potting mix for the container garden using the same ingredients as the seedling-starting mix. But you can use regular compost with a coarser texture.

LETTUCE

Even small pots can be heavy and difficult to move when full of soil. So it's best to move the containers to their final location and fill them in place.

Leave at least an inch of space between the soil and the top of the container.

This will keep water from pouring off the surface.

1 inch

When can we plant the seeds?

According to the package, lettuce seeds can germinate in temperatures as low as forty-five degrees Fahrenheit.

LETTUCE

Use a min-max thermometer to keep track of the temperatures inside the cold frame. Check the readings daily and reset the thermometer in the evenings.

Record each day's highest and lowest temperatures. When the low temperature is above forty-five degrees Fahrenheit for a few days, then it's warm enough to plant lettuce seeds.

45° F low temp

The seed package will provide guidelines for sowing lettuce seeds. A good method for planting leaf lettuce seeds in a container garden is called broadcast sowing.

You simply scatter the tiny seeds evenly over the surface of the potting mix. Cover the seeds with an additional 1/4 inch of mix. Be careful not to bury them too deeply or they won't germinate.

Keep the seeds moist by watering them every other day until they sprout.

LETTUCE

He said I didn't appreciate his genius and kicked me out of the greenhouse.

I haven't seen him since.

Maybe the plant ate him? We should check and see if he's okay.

That doesn't sound good.

I agree.

Darn...

The door is still locked.

But look, there's a place for the medallion here, too.

You're right! It fits perfectly.

You did it!

We can go in!

Where did you find this?

Wrigley ate it when he was living in the compost bin.

Careful, these are some of the carnivorous plants I was talking about.

They *are* big enough to catch a gnome.

Ivy, is that you?

Uh...hi! How's it going, Mr. Thorn?

How did you get in?

We have this magical treasure that opens doors and does other cool stuff.

Magic? Give that to me.

Interesting... It's some sort of powerful gnome artifact. This might be what I've needed to complete my secret project.

Hey! Give it back.

I will use its magic to revivify my new collection of carnivorous plants. Then no one can stop me from taking over the school. Not even Marvin in his robot suit!

Are you okay?

I'm fine thanks to your quick thinking and the power of the super shovel.

Not only did you find my shovel's missing piece but you worked together to save me. You also helped each other grow seedlings, made compost, created potting mix, and selected garden containers as a team. You proved that you deserve to be official members of the *Green Hat Garden Gnomes*.

You can do that?

Yes. I started this school to find new recruits.

That's why the super shovel symbol is everywhere.

Here are your new green hats.

Whoa!

You saved me from becoming a pitcher plant snack *and* protected the school from Mr. Thorn's terrible topiary, *but*...

you're not done yet.

Ouchy!

Your first task as Green Hat Gnomes is to plant a container garden.

PLANT YOUR OWN *Container*

You can do it!

Things needed for a container garden:

digging tools:

spoon

trowel

containers with good drainage (see page 100)

potting mix (see page 57)

POTTING MIX

plant supports

tomato cage or bamboo poles or wooden stakes

hardened-off seedlings ready to transplant (see page 105)

seeds to sow directly into the garden

Check your local forecast to determine when the weather will be warm enough to plant the garden outside.

FORECAST

HIGH 68° LOW 54°

HIGH 65° LOW 53°

HIGH 73° LOW 56°

MON   TUES

Dig a hole large enough for the transplant's entire root ball.

Most seedlings should be planted at the same depth as they were in their pots.

But tomato transplants like having some of their stem buried.

remove bottom leaves

bury stem

After planting the seedlings, install supports for tall or climbing plants like tomatoes.

Give newly transplanted sprouts a good watering. Use a gentle shower to avoid disturbing the soil.

Stop watering when liquid starts to leak out from the drainage holes.

Empty any water collecting in trays sitting beneath the containers. Do not let them stand in pools of water.

Now that we're done transplanting the seedlings, let's plant some seeds.

Many vegetables, like beans, carrots, and lettuce, can be sown directly into the garden when the weather is warm. The seed package will describe the optimum weather conditions for planting the seeds outside.

Bush Beans

spacing 2-4 in.

planting depth 1 inch

Sowing Instructions:
Plant directly in the garden after all danger of frost has passed. Seeds will not germinate well in soil temperatures below sixty degrees Fahrenheit.

Direct Seeding: Plant seeds one inch deep, two to four inches apart, in rows eighteen to thirty-six inches apart.

Sowing seeds in a container garden is slightly different from planting a traditional garden. Traditional gardens are laid out in rows. Gardeners walk down the rows between plants to tend to the crops and harvest vegetables.

space → between rows

Container plants are accessible from all sides, so there's no need to plant seeds in rows.

easy access for harvesting and plant care

The sowing instructions on seed packages provide measurements for the spacing between plants.

Measure the spacing between the seeds you sow. Keep them the same distance away from the side of the containers, too.

Bush Beans

If you're having difficulty determining seed spacing, here are general measurements to use for a few popular crops:

Bush Beans

Bush Beans:
    2-4 inches apart
Broccoli:
    10 inches apart
Carrots:
    1-2 inches apart
Cucumbers:
    8-10 inches apart
Lettuce:
    4-9 inches apart
Peppers:
    8-10 inches apart
Squash:
    12-20 inches apart
Tomatoes:
    12-20 inches apart

As the garden grows, it will start attracting unwanted visitors looking for a snack.

This looks delicious!

Insecticidal soap is an organic product that can be effective against soft-bodied pests like aphids, leafhoppers, mealybugs, thrips, scale insects, spider mites, whiteflies, and others.

Commercially available insecticidal soaps contain potassium hydroxide and fatty acids to kill insects. These products are safe to use on most plants. You can make your own insecticidal soap, but be careful. Using the wrong soap or too much of it can harm plants.

SAFE INSECT KILLING SOAP

Insecticidal soap recipe:

1. Mix 2 teaspoons of liquid castile soap with one quart of water. Other types of soap can harm plants.

2. Put mixture into a spray bottle.

Test the spray on a few leaves first. Then apply to areas infested by pests. Spray both sides of leaves.

Insecticidal soap works on contact. You need to cover the insects to be effective. Reapply to infested plants once a week.

This soap can also help wash away sooty mold.

Spritz pests on the underside of leaves, too!

Some plants can be sensitive to insecticidal soap. Rinse plants with water if leaves begin to wilt and turn brown. Never spray blooms or flowers.

The spray won't deter all hungry visitors. Sometimes, you just have to remove pests from your garden by hand.

slug

tomato hornworm

If the idea of touching slugs grosses you out, try these other methods to keep them away from the garden.

Water in the morning. This gives surface moisture time to evaporate during the day and makes the garden less hospitable to hungry slugs at night.

Cover the soil with lava rocks.* Slugs don't like crawling over these rough rocks. Make a ring of rocks around the base of the plant. Be careful to avoid crushing or harming the stem.

Ouch.

Or surround the plants with fresh coffee grounds.

Slugs don't like caffeine.

Yuck.

Whew, planting a garden is a lot of work.

Even a small gnome-sized one like this.

But all the time and energy we've spent growing strong seedlings, preparing good potting mix, and finding the sunniest spot for the garden will be worth it when we harvest our first crop of vegetables.

*You can buy lava rocks at gardening supply stores.

You don't need access to Marvin's secret storage facility.
Here are a few highly regarded seed suppliers you can order from.

Fedco Seeds—fedcoseeds.com/seeds

Based in Maine, Fedco is a good source for cold-hardy vegetables well suited for areas with a cooler climate like the Northeast. Their large selection of certified organic and heirloom seeds is available online.

High Mowing Seeds—highmowingseeds.com

High Mowing Seeds is a company with a strong focus on sustainable gardening and is a verified fully organic seed company.

Southern Exposure Seed Exchange—southernexposure.com

Located in Virginia, this company offers many varieties of heirloom and organic vegetable seeds. They emphasize varieties that perform well in the mid-Atlantic and Southeast.

handy conversion tables

For K and C
Together we grow!

First Second

All instructions included in this book are provided as a resource for parents and children.
While all due care has been taken, we recommend that an adult supervise children at
all times when following the instructions in this book. The projects in this book are not
recommended for children three years and under due to potential choking hazard. Neither
the authors nor the publisher accept any responsibility for any loss, injury, or damages
sustained by anyone resulting from the instructions contained in this book.

Published by First Second
First Second is an imprint of Roaring Brook Press,
a division of Holtzbrinck Publishing Holdings Limited Partnership
120 Broadway, New York, NY 10271

Don't miss your next favorite book from First Second! For the latest updates go to
firstsecondnewsletter.com and sign up for our enewsletter.

Library of Congress Control Number: 2019930671

Paperback ISBN: 978-1-250-15214-5
Hardcover ISBN: 978-1-250-15213-8

Our books may be purchased in bulk for promotional, educational, or business use.
Please contact your local bookseller or the Macmillan Corporate and Premium Sales Department
at (800) 221-7945 ext. 5442 or by email at MacmillanSpecialMarkets@macmillan.com.

First edition, 2020
Edited by Robyn Chapman and Bethany Bryan
Expert consultation by Margaret Roach
Cover design by Andrew Arnold
Interior book design by Alexis Frederick-Frost and Rob Steen

Printed in China by 1010 Printing International Limited, North Point, Hong Kong

Created in Photoshop. Inked digitally using a Wacom Intuos tablet and stylus with flex nib and Kyle Webster's
Classic Cartoonist digital brush. Colored with Kyle Webster's PRO comics inker digital brush.

Paperback: 10 9 8 7 6 5 4 3 2 1
Hardcover: 10 9 8 7 6 5 4 3 2 1